WELCOME HOMES

THE JOY OF ENTERTAINING

C.R.Gibson®
FINE GIFTS SINCE 1870

DECIDING ON THE OCCASIO

EXOTIC EVENING

All these dishes are subtly spiced to give a well-balanced and exotic menu. Serves 6

PEPPERED SCALLOPS
Two colorful sauces accompany the peppery scallops.

LAMB TAGINE WITH COUSCOUS
Tender young lamb stuffed with a piquant-sweet mix of spices, herbs, and prunes.

COCONUT & SAFFRON ICE CREAM
A dreamy, creamy concoction with flavors and textures that are irresistible.

DRINKS
An oaky, buttery New World Chardonnay complements the scallops, and a full, rich, spicy Australian Shiraz, served with the tagine, is ideal. Serve a chilled sweet white port with the ice cream.

PLANNING NOTES
The ice cream can be made up to six weeks ahead. Prepare the stuffing for the lamb tagine in advance, if necessary. The two sauces for the scallops can be prepared ahead of time, kept covered with plastic wrap in the refrigerator, then heated for serving.

IDEAL PARTNERS
Always make sure that the food you serve suits the occasion and looks impressive with the table decorations you choose.

WHETHER THE DECISION TO ENTERTAIN springs from a simple desire to have a party, or you have some friends you would like to see, planning a event, in my mind, is as important as the event itself.

If it begins with the guests, how best to entertain them? Would they prefer a lazy lunch, an elegant dinner, a summer barbecue, or a refined tea? On the other hand, if your motivation is the occasion itself, you will need t decide on a guest list to suit the event. I always try to assemble a group tha has at least one linking thread of interest and invite a good conversationalist Also consider any restraints: how much time and expense can you spare? How much room (including oven and refrigerator space) do you have, and are you confident in catering to and entertaining large numbers?

TAKING CARE OF THE DETAILS

I find a party is easier to orchestrate if I plan it around a theme, perhaps dictated by the food I serve or the season: a vegetarian winter supper, an Italian buffet, or a summer barbecue. Plan the table setting and food presentation, remembering that small touches make all the difference.

COUNTRY HAMPER
PICNIC

FESTIVE CELEBRATION
DINNER

CHAMPAGNE
BUFFET

ntertaining is the very stuff of life

nviting your guests can usually be done informally over the telephone. This
ften means an instant reply and gives you the opportunity to inquire about
ood dislikes or allergies. If you wish, send written invitations to make it
nore of an event. Remember to include a dress code, particularly if your
heme requires it, as well as the reason for the party if it is a celebration.

WHAT FOOD TO SERVE

he key to every successful menu is balance: choose
nteresting ingredients, and consider how their flavors,
olors, and textures interact with one another. Bear
n mind that the freshest ingredients in season are
lways the best. It is simple to mix and match different
ecipes, as long as you always remember that no two
ourses should be too rich. Never take on too much;
t is essential that you are relaxed and at ease while
ou cook and entertain. Your guests will be able to
ense if you are not.

CONSIDER YOUR DRINKS

he type of occasion and the
ood you plan to serve are
mportant considerations when
eciding what to drink with
our meal: a refined wine and
iery barbecue food will not do
ustice to each other. Serving
n aperitif before the meal is a
great way to relax your friends,
ut do make sure it is not so
strong that it spoils the first
course. A brandy, liqueur, or
port with coffee after the meal
is also welcome, especially in
winter. When calculating how
much wine to buy, I usually
allow, on average, three glasses
per person with the meal.
Always stock up on mineral
water and one soda alternative.

*D*ining with your
family is a daily
time for relaxing, sharing,
and bonding. Dining with
your friends and relatives is
an occasion for celebration,
regardless of the event or
season. Don't fret over the
details; instead embrace this
as an opportunity to share
your creativity and
hospitality with others.

3

FLOWERS TO IMPRESS   A daisy

ARRANGING FLOWERS
Do this well ahead, leaving you time to perfect the food.

SCHEDULE
Buy flowers about three days in advance, condition them, and store in buckets until you are ready to arrange them.

> *T*he most beautiful adornments are not fashioned by hand but are the handiwork of the sun and rain in Nature's workshop.

THE PRESENCE OF FLOWERS lends a grace to any and every occasion. Choose your flowers carefully, then take the time to condition them to make sure they look at their best for your party. A few basic items of equipment are essential. For informal displays, you will need a good pair of florists' scissors, a pair of pruners for cutting woody stems, a small, sharp knife for scraping stems, and buckets in which to condition flowers (use pitchers or vases for smaller flowers). For more complex arrangements, you may need florists' foam, chicken wire, stub wires, wire cutters, florists' gum, and prongs.

FLOWER CHOICE

First decide on the type of arrangement (or arrangements) you want at your party. Where would you like to display it? How much space is available? What vases or other receptacles do you have? What flowers are in season? Do they tie in with, or can they dictate your color scheme? Low displays are most suitable for the table, but larger bold ones can really impress; either have one on the dining table until guests sit down to eat or place on a side table or mantelpiece. Gain inspiration from the gallery on the right, which

INDIVIDUAL TREATMENT

All flowers and foliage should be conditioned as described opposite, but certain plant types need additional special treatment. The hard stems of woody shrubs must be cut at an angle as usual, then the base of each stem split up center, so it takes up water more efficiently. Scrape 2in (5cm) of the bark as usual.

Milky-sapped plants, such as euphorbia and poppy, need to be seared in a flame once cut to stop them from weeping. Cut flowers may have been seared by the florist already.

Some plants, most notably tulips, Corsican hellebore, and privet, are so acidic they adversely affect other flowers so are best displayed alone.

very bit as beautiful as an orchid

hows a wide range of floral displays, for ideas
or table, individual place setting, side table, wall,
nd mantelpiece arrangements.

CONDITIONING

usually buy flowers three days in advance of the
ccasion, selecting specimens that are just beyond
he bud stage, with healthy fresh leaves. Check
tems that have been underwater are not white or
ale and are free of slimy bacteria.

When you return home, prepare all plant
naterial by cutting the ends of the stems at a sharp
ingle and scraping 2in (5cm) around each stem up
rom the base. Remove any leaves that will be
ubmerged in the final arrangement, and plunge the
lowers or foliage into a bucket of water with three
or four drops of household bleach added (this
nhibits the bacteria that causes plants to rot). Leave
n a cool, light (not sunny) place for at least two
nours, but preferably overnight or until buds have
opened and you do the arrangement, ideally the day
before the event. Keep the buckets in a cool place to
prolong the plant material's life.

Once arranged, change the water regularly,
adding a few drops of bleach each time. Drooping
stems are sometimes revived by placing their ends
nto almost boiling water for five to ten minutes.

FLOWER GALLERY

LIGHTING

THE NATURE AND LEVEL of lighting plays a key role in creating the right atmosphere for your entertainment – it can definitely make or break an occasion. During the day you have less control; though inside, blinds are effective for shading intrusive rays of sun through windows, and on gloomy days candlelight can be most welcome. Outside, for the sake of both guests and the food, the area where you sit and eat should be shaded. Some of my most memorable meals have been enjoyed outside in the soft dappled shade of a vine canopy.

CANDLE EFFECT

In the evening, candles give a soft and flattering light that creates an easy ambience in which people seem to flourish. Candlelight alone may not be sufficient to serve and eat by, so add a little gentle electric illumination to make sure the level of brightness feels just right.

Besides using candlesticks and candelabras, consider including candles in floral displays, or make lanterns. Outside, candles need to be protected from a breeze. Although glass candle protectors are readily available, you can improvise your own by placing candles in drinking glasses. Remember that scented candles, such as rosemary, citronella, and lemon, are excellent at keeping insects away.

TABLE DISPLAYS

CANDLE SAFETY

Never leave candles burning unattended. Inside, in particular, light candles only when someone can keep an eye on them. Position them carefully out of the way of individuals serving food, where they will not impede the view across the table, or scorch flower arrangements or walls.

Candles used in displays with fresh flowers are moderately safe because the plant material is unlikely to catch fire, and the container has water in it. Make sure that the candles are always taller than or well away from flowers and leaves.

TABLE LINEN

THE MOST INVITING dinner tables I have seen often owe much of their appeal to the table linen: the cloth and the napkins. Consider the color of the cloth carefully as it dominates the look of the table; I believe in keeping it plain. If you are buying new table linen, neutral colors are the most useful; white, cream, and pale gray are all favorites of mine, but of the darker colors, holly green and rich dark red can look magnificent, especially in winter. Wooden table surfaces are soft and mellow, but it is most important to use place mats to prevent scratches and heat damage to the table. Choose them to co-ordinate with the table decorations and napkins.

THE DETAILS

Much old-fashioned formality has now disappeared, but I am always disappointed if I do not have a crisply laundered plain or damask linen napkin in a restaurant. Cloth napkins engender a great sense of luxury at home, too, and although they may involve more work afterward, their contribution to the overall effect makes them well worth the effort for the majority of occasions. For large parties, paper napkins are more practical, though. I prefer a simple rolled or folded napkin, maybe with a decorative ring or tie.

NAPKIN IDEAS

NAPKIN RINGS

Use braided raffia or ribbon, wire-edged for best effect, to make your own napkin rings. It is very simple, and is a most effective way of linking the assorted decorative elements of your table together.

The smallest details often require the greatest attention.

THE PLACE SETTING Fortunatel

A NAGGING BUT UNNECESSARY CONCERN often surrounds the order in which cutlery should be placed when setting a dining table. The simple convention (below) is that knives, forks, and spoons are placed in course order, from the outside inward, on either side of a central plate. A bread knife is placed on the extreme right. Water and wine glasses stand on the right above the knives, and the side plate with its napkin sits on the left beyond the cutlery. An alternative, particularly if the napkin is decoratively folded or tied (page 7), is to place it on the central plate, with the bread knife on the side plate. If this layout takes up too much space around your table, consider one of the more informal options (right).

FORMAL SETTING
This setting is for four courses: soup, then a savory first course, followed by the main course, and a dessert. Two wines will be served. A charger plate adds to the formality of the setting.

Formality and informality serve the same purpose: To create an atmosphere for your guests that compliments the purpose of your celebration.

SIDE PLATE
Placed to the left of the main plate, this often has the napkin on it, and is used for bread or salad.

CHARGER PLATE
An optional large decorative plate remains in place throughout the meal.

ating peas off a knife is not easy

WINE GLASSES
The glass used first, usually for white wine, is closest to the plate.

WATER GLASS
Place this above the knives.

ALTERNATE LAYOUT

Table settings can easily be adapted from the conventional one (left) for less formal occasions and to limit the amount of lateral space occupied by each place, perhaps when entertaining more than six people around the average-sized dining table. Two possible alternatives are shown below.

CUTLERY
Arrange in the order of the courses, from the outside in, with extras such as the bread knife on the outside.

INFORMAL SETTING
Here, the dessert spoon and fork are set above the plate, spoon above fork, with the handles pointing in the direction in which they will be picked up. Place the napkin on the central plate or side plate.

MINIMALIST
Unless the first course and the main course are too divergent in flavor, use the same knife and fork for both. A cutlery rest helps keep the table clean. Use an informal wine glass for wine or water.

COUNTDOWN TO THE EVEN[T]

FIRST DRINKS
Set out drinks and glasses in readiness for pouring as soon as your guests arrive.

SHOPPING
Plan to shop more than once; this allows you to purchase items that were unavailable or that you may have forgotten to buy first time around.

THE KEY TO KEEPING CALM is having everything well ordered. You will feel much more at ease and, consequently, so will your guests. Making lists may sound dull but, when organizing an event, I cannot do without them.

DECISIONS, LISTS, AND SCHEDULES

Once you have chosen a menu and settled on a theme, make a shopping list of all the ingredients needed, including drinks to be ordered, remembering nonalcoholic drinks, and tea and coffee. Decide on flowers or other special items like candles that you may require and add these to your shopping list. Next, plan a detailed cooking schedule, always including early preparation tasks such as marinating.

Now is the time to consider the format of the actual occasion itself. Plan exactly where each stage of the event should take place, from premeal drinks to coffee afterward. When this is decided, make a second schedule of noncooking tasks such as arranging flowers, preparing any special items, setting the table, tidying up, and drawing up a seating plan. Include on this list reminders of tasks to be done during the event, too, such as adjusting the central heating, preheating the oven, or removing sorbet from the freezer to soften. Closer to the event, it may help to combine your cooking and noncooking schedules.

"Perfection is the chil[d]

10

THE TIME APPROACHES

While cooking, I frequently find a second timer is a useful reminder of noncooking tasks that still need to be completed. Try, if you can, to leave plenty of time for any glitches, as well as a restorative tea or coffee break. Strike out the jobs on your lists as you complete them – this is both satisfying and reassuring.

Make sure that each space you will be using is neat and welcoming, and set up what you need in each room before everyone arrives. Set a drink tray in readiness, and place cups and saucers where you plan to serve coffee. Decide on a division of tasks if more than one of you is hosting the event.

LAST-MINUTE PANIC

Remember to allow enough time to get yourself ready. There is bound to be some last-minute cooking, however much you prepare in advance, but a few minutes of relaxation with a drink before the doorbell rings is a lifesaver.

SCHEDULE

▷ SEVERAL WEEKS BEFORE
Decide to have a party
Consider who to invite
Issue invitations
Choose a menu
Hire any help or rent necessary equipment

▷ THE WEEK BEFORE
Prepare food, drink, and flowers shopping list
Write out party schedule
Cook food that can be frozen
Decide rooms in which you will entertain

▷ THREE DAYS BEFORE
Buy and condition flowers
Make relevant table decorations
Buy drinks

▷ THE PREVIOUS DAY
Shop for food
Arrange flowers
Tidy up and iron table linen
Make sure you have a good supply of ice
Prepare food that can be kept overnight

▷ THE DAY OF THE PARTY
Prepare as much food in advance as possible
Do all cooking that can be reheated
   at the last minute
Prepare rooms where you will be entertaining
Set out drink tray
Bring wines to correct temperatures

▷ A FEW HOURS BEFORE
Set table
Decide on seating plan
Start any early cooking

▷ THE LAST HOUR
Have as much cooking as possible underway
Straighten up kitchen; wash dishes
Get yourself ready
Open red wines to breathe
Take a short break – you deserve it!

▷ AT THE PARTY
For lunch or dinner parties, allow 1¼ hours
from the first guest arriving to starting the meal

The best laid plans ... almost always work out just fine.

f time." JOSEPH HALL 1574–1656

BREAKFAST & BRUNCH

THE FIRST MEAL OF THE DAY IS A PARTICULAR AND SPECIAL ONE, AWAKENING APPETITES ANEW. SERVED AS A HEARTY FAMILY FEAST, A SPREAD FOR A CASUAL GATHERING OF FRIENDS, OR AN INTIMATE REPAST FOR TWO, IT SHOULD ALWAYS BE HOMEY, RELAXED, AND INFORMAL. THE DISHES ARE ONES OF WHICH WE NEVER TIRE: I SO RELISH THE TASTE-PACKED MIX OF THESE SIMPLE FOODS THAT I AM OFTEN TEMPTED TO PREPARE THEM FOR LUNCH AND DINNER, TOO!

A rustic outdoor setting (right) provides the perfect context for the delicious flavors of a late summer brunch.

INDULGENT

Breakfast together, companions forever

FOR A LUXURIANT and intimate breakfast in bed, set trays in advance, have the brioche ready to warm, champagne chilled, and the coffeepot waiting.

LOVER'S ROSE HEART
Ensure a romantic start to the day by making a simple, sweet-scented heart to grace the breakfast tray. Moss frames the flowers, and galax leaves adorn the sides.

CAFETIERE
Be sure to make enough richly aromatic coffee for two cups each.

1 Wrap the base and sides of a piece of soaked florists' foam in plastic. Trim the plastic to fit, and secure with adhesive tape.

2 Cut one side of each galax leaf straight, to align with the base of the foam. Apply glue along the straight edge.

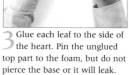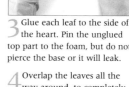

3 Glue each leaf to the side of the heart. Pin the unglued top part to the foam, but do not pierce the base or it will leak.

4 Overlap the leaves all the way around, to completely cover the sides. Trim the rose stems to 1in (2.5cm) each, and stick in the center of the foam shape. Tuck a ruff of Spanish moss between the leaves and roses to finish the heart.

Secure moss and stray leaves with pins

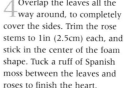

*A romantic breakfast
with your spouse
will fill your hearts
and nourish your marriage.*

ROSE IN A NAPKIN
*Fold a large linen napkin
into a triangle, then wrap
it around a single rose.*

LINEN TRAY CLOTH
*As a tray cloth, use a linen
napkin that matches the
one holding the rose.*

LEMON CURD
*Spoon an individual
portion of homemade
lemon curd into a small
bowl for the tray.*

L U N C H

RELAXING MEALS IN THE MIDDLE OF THE DAY ARE ALL TOO OFTEN NEGLECTED, THANKS TO THE HECTIC PACE OF MODERN LIVING. YET THEY CAN BE ONE OF LIFE'S GREAT PLEASURES, SINCE OUR APPETITES ARE AT THEIR SHARPEST AT NOON. THE WEEKEND BECOMES IDEAL FOR A SIMPLE BUT DELICIOUS MEAL WITH FAMILY AND FRIENDS. ONCE FOOD AND WINE HAVE BEEN SAVORED, PLENTY OF TIME IS LEFT FOR INDULGING IN LEISURELY CONVERSATION, A WALK, OR EVEN A SIESTA.

  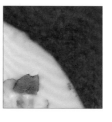

For a tempting, exotic lunch party, team the interesting textures and spicy tastes of the Orient with cheerful flowers and vibrant colors (right).

VIBRANT

Never neglect color. It plays an importar

THE COLOR of both food and tableware affects our enjoyment of meals more than we might imagine: vibrant colors set our taste buds tingling. Entertain colorfully, and your meals will always be memorable.

Phlox

Ranunculus

Rose

Selaginella

FLOATING FLOWERS

Place shallow bowls of floating, brightly colored flowers on the table where they will not interrupt your view. Choose flowers and foliage in vivid colors that contrast and clash excitingly. Here, I have used ferny selaginella and roses in an etched, black glass bowl.

CONTRAST
Note how much the effect changes when flowers of different colors are used. Try alternative varieties to tie in with your own setting.

1 Trim off the leafy stems, leaving about ½in (1cm). If necessary, make small bunches by tying 3–4 stems together.

2 Cut each of the flower stems just below the base of its flowerhead. Be careful not to dislodge the petals.

3 Fill a shallow bowl with water. Place foliage bunches in first, then position your flowers (above left).

art in the enjoyment of food

FLOWER SETTINGS
Small bowls with roses, gerbera, and fern leaves are arranged at each place setting to echo the main display.

BOLD NAPKINS
When tied in a bow with pink wire-edged ribbon, blue linen napkins are brightened even more.

PATTERNED TABLECLOTH
As demonstrated by the faux tapestry cloth that sets the color theme for the china, tablecloths need not always form a neutral backdrop.

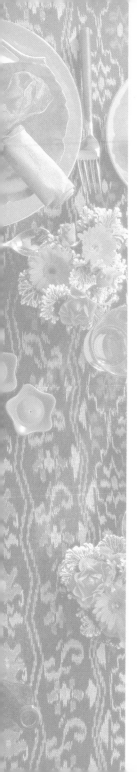

DINNER

EVENING HAS TO BE THE OPTIMUM TIME TO ENTERTAIN. WORK AND OTHER DAYTIME ACTIVITIES ARE OVER, PEOPLE ARE ALL READY TO WIND DOWN AND LET THE DAY'S PRESSURES RECEDE. APPETITES ARE SHARP, AND WE LOOK FORWARD TO BEING SOCIABLE. SO SEND OUT INVITATIONS, SELECT A TANTALIZING MENU, ADORN THE DINING TABLE, PREPARE SUMPTUOUS FOOD AND DRINKS, AND JOIN YOUR GUESTS IN STIMULATING CONVERSATION.

Prepare festive celebration foods for a rich and colorful Carnival party (right) at which you and all your guests wear masks.

FIRESIDE

"... intimate delights, fireside enjoyment

GOOD FOOD in an atmosphere of warmth and comfort gives rise to superb conversation. Lighted candles and a crackling fire ensure an enjoyable supper.

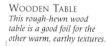

WOODEN TABLE
This rough-hewn wood table is a good foil for the other warm, earthy textures.

CANDLE BASKET
Flowers, seeds, nuts, and spices mingle with similarly colored candles in this box of delight. Never leave lit candles unattended.

*T*he best light illuminates
the room ...

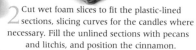

1 Line three sections of a cutlery basket with plastic. Place four candles at random, securing with adhesive putty. Tie a bundle of cinnamon with raffia.

2 Cut wet foam slices to fit the plastic-lined sections, slicing curves for the candles where necessary. Fill the unlined sections with pecans and litchis, and position the cinnamon.

3 Push fresh roses and coneflowers, with stems cut to 1in (2.5cm) long, into the wet foam to form a dense cover. Fill in with pecans and litchis, to complete the display (top). Dampen the foam so the flowers last.

22

... and captures the glow of
those who share your table.

ome-born happiness." WILLIAM COWPER 1731–1800

CINNAMON CANDLE
Stand a candle with a cinnamon-stick fence at each place. To make the fence, tie a loop at the middle of a length of string, then tie the sticks on behind. Make a bow through the loop when the fence is long enough.

CUTLERY REST
To encourage informality, use the same cutlery for all the savory dishes. A tripod of cinnamon sticks tied with string forms an attractive resting place for the cutlery between courses.

BUFFET
PARTIES

WINING AND DINING MORE THAN TWELVE GUESTS IS MOST EASILY EXECUTED WITH A BUFFET. THERE ARE PLENTY OF EASY DISHES YOU CAN PREPARE WELL IN ADVANCE OR, IF YOU PREFER TO LIVE DANGEROUSLY, AFTER YOUR GUESTS HAVE ARRIVED! PLAN AND ADHERE TO A METICULOUS WORK SCHEDULE, COOK FLAVORFUL FOOD THAT IS SIMPLE TO EAT, AND A RELAXED AND SOCIABLE CELEBRATION WILL BE ASSURED.

A champagne buffet, with such flavorsome foods as marinated salmon, chicken crepe stack, and savarin, is especially appropriate for Christmas celebrations (right).

ALFRESCO

"The greatest dishes are very simple dishe

WHEN THE WEATHER IS FAIR, serve an appetizing and relaxed buffet lunch outdoors in your garden. Set it up out of the sun but near the house, so that hot food does not cool too much on its way to the table.

BUFFET TABLE
The table is informally laid for guest to help themselves to all courses. Win and glasses are to one side, away from the food, for easy replenishmen

ICE BOWL
Very beautiful, yet simple to make, ice bowls last for over an hour in the shade, once out of the freezer. Choose plants that are in season.

Alstroemeria _____ _____ Sweet pea

Eustoma

St. John's wort

1 Place one bowl inside another 1¼–1¾ in (3–4cm) larger in diameter. Half fill the outer bowl with water, adding a little milk or food coloring for a frosted effect.

2 Gently fill the inner bowl with water so that it sinks to the same level as the outer bowl. Hold it straight in a central position, and secure with adhesive tape.

3 Wedge nontoxic plant material into the water. Freeze for at least 8 hours. To release, pour cold water into the inner bowl, and partially submerge the outer bowl in cold, never warm, water. After a minute, ease the ice bowl free.

GEORGE AUGUSTE ESCOFFIER 1846–1935

CHILI POT
Fill little terra-cotta pots with chilies emerging from a ruff of foliage, their ends fanned out like a fountain. Being small, these pots do not clutter the table.

FROSTED SERVING BOWL
An ice bowl is a fitting and attractive receptacle from which to serve sorbet and ice cream. Fill with scoops of softened ice cream just before serving.

With the sky as your canopy and the grass as your carpet, conversation and laughter will be freed to fill the open spaces.

COCKTAIL PARTIES

DEVILISH DRINKS SERVED IN ELEGANT GLASSES WITH PLATTERS OF DELECTABLE SAVORIES, ALL AGAINST AN IMPRESSIVE BACKDROP OF HIGHLY POLISHED SILVERWARE AND EXQUISITE FLOWERS: THESE ARE THE EXCITING ELEMENTS THAT MAKE UP THAT MOST GLAMOROUS OF OCCASIONS, THE COCKTAIL PARTY. THIS SHOULD NOT BE A TIME TO HOLD BACK: FOR A SENSATION-PACKED EVENT, MAKE SURE THAT YOU PULL OUT ALL THE STOPS.

Create a thrilling atmosphere with bold arrangements of flowers (right), wickedly indulgent drinks, and imaginative cocktail food.

GLAMOUR

"I can resist everything except temptation"

LIVELY PRESENTATION with a sophisticated atmosphere will guarantee that both old-time favorites and exotic delicacies are impossible to resist.

FLOWERS AND CANDLES

A low arrangement becomes even more effective when it includes candles. For safety, be sure the lit candles are taller than any plant material in the basket.

Ranunculus

Snapdragon

Tulip

Rose

Orchid

Ivy

1 Line a basket, or other low container, with plastic. Place the candles and secure with clay. Fill the basket with soaked florists' foam, cutting it to fit around the candles. Place trailing foliage, such as ivy, around the edges.

2 Cut the flower stems to 2½ in (6cm). Insert them so they protrude about 1in (2.5cm) above the edge of the container. Arrange them in bands of color, as the roses are here.

3 Keep the color bands quite informal and fill in gaps with "pools" of flowers, hiding all the foam and plastic to complete the arrangement (above right).

SCAR WILDE 1854–1900

DRINK TRAY
A polished silver tray reflects the
glasses and their exciting contents,
showing them off to great advantage.

BOLD PLATTER
Brilliant red plates echo the vibrant
colors of some of the cocktails, the
food, and the basket of flowers.

COCKTAIL NAPKINS
When eating finger food, small
napkins (linen for greatest luxury)
are essential. Arrange a pile on
the table within easy reach.

Glamour is not a lost art, it simply requires a slight nudge to awaken in the imagination of those who want to share their home with others.

BARBECUES

FEW SENSATIONS SET OUR TASTE BUDS TINGLING LIKE THE WONDERFUL AROMA OF OUTDOOR COOKING AND THE UNIQUE FLAVOR OF A BARBECUED MEAL. GLOWING WOOD AND COALS COOK MANY FOODS SUPERBLY. ADD TO THIS THE DELIGHT OF ALFRESCO LUNCHES ON WARM SUMMER DAYS OR EVENING ENTERTAINING UNDER A STARLIT SKY AND, LIKE ME, YOU WILL BE BARBECUING MORE AND MORE, SOMETIMES EVEN IN THE MIDDLE OF WINTER.

Enjoy aromatic grilled fish and seafood dishes by moon and lantern light (right). These foods cook extremely well on the barbecue.

DAYTIME

Simple country food is best in the open a

MAKE SIMPLICITY your goal when setting the
table outside for a lunchtime barbecue.
Concentrate on comfort
and relaxed informality.

INSTANT WINDOW BOX

Fill a wooden box with small
potted plants and cut flowers.
Use miniature roses in pots as
the backbone, and fill in with cut
flowers such as these anemones,
sweet peas, and pittosporum.

FLOWER NAPKIN RING
*Tuck a bold flower between
each napkin and its ring.
Choose blooms that do not
wilt quickly.*

1 Completely line a wooden box
with a plastic trash bag. Wrap and
tape up the rose pots, too, to prevent
their roots from becoming waterlogged.

2 Place the pots
in first, then wedge in soaked florists'
foam, carved to fit around the plastic
covered pots. Trim overlapping plastic.

3 Insert the other flowers and foliage into
the foam around the roses, keeping the
stems fairly upright to simulate natural
growth. Be sure the foam is hidden (see
finished box above). To prolong the display,
replace wilted flowers, and keep foam moist.

FINGER BOWL
*A bowl of warm water with
citrus slices for finger-dipping
is a thoughtful gesture beside
each setting at a barbecue.*

BEAUTIFUL FLOWERS
*Brighten up the table with
a simple earthenware vase
of flowers that echo the
ones in the window box.*

A successful barbecue
requires a juicy
cut of meat, a tangy sauce,
and an inexhaustible supply
of napkins.

COFFEE
MORNINGS
& AFTERNOON TEA

IN DAYS GONE BY, PEOPLE SEEMED TO HAVE THE TIME TO STOP FOR MORNING COFFEE OR AFTERNOON TEA. NOW, MOST OF US ARE TOO BUSY FOR MORE THAN A QUICK DRINK IN BETWEEN MAIN MEALS. SURELY IT IS TIME TO REVIVE THE CUSTOM, EVEN IF ONLY ON WEEKENDS, SO WITH FAMILY AND FRIENDS WE CAN ENJOY ONCE AGAIN THOSE DELICIOUS SCONES, MOIST CAKES, AND SANDWICHES.

Long-established teatime favorites like lemon sponge cake, shortbread, and crumpets should be served on delicate china (right).

COTTAGE

"'How long does getting thin

RE-CREATE CHILDHOOD MEMORIES with pastel colored floral china, feather-light cakes with pretty icing, flowers, and, of course, many cups of restorative tea.

FLOWER VASE
Seasonal flowers in a cream-colored vase are most effective.

A fternoon tea fueled the imagination of Shakespeare and the resolve of Churchill ...

CRYSTALLIZED PETALS

Decorate iced cakes with edible sugared rose petals to match your tableware. Arrange them to resemble flowers or just scatter on the cake.

1 Carefully remove petals from rose flowerheads and paint both sides of each one with lightly beaten egg white.

2 Use a tea strainer or small sieve to sprinkle both sides of each petal with superfine sugar before the egg white dries.

CHOCOLATE LEAVES

Turn an iced cake into a feast for the eyes by decorating it with an extravagant bow and leaves made using your favorite kind of chocolate.

1 Melt chocolate until it is viscous but not runny. Paint it smoothly on one side of a firm, clean leaf.

2 Chill the chocolate until se then gently peel the leaves off. Place among ribbons and bows as shown below.

FLORAL THEME
Arrange the sugared petals to resemble a flower. The green calyx is purely decorative and should not be eaten.

TRIMMING
Tie two lengths of si ribbon in a sumptuo bow to make a enticing packag

… but its greatest contribution is to quiet the mind at the end of a busy day.

take?' Pooh asked anxiously." A.A. MILNE 1882–1956

DISHES
Evoke the mood of bygone days with fine floral china.

CAKE
Pink and yellow petals on a sponge cake continue a cottage garden theme.

ACE TABLECLOTH
elicately flowered lace orks very well with aditional china.

This book is based on *Entertaining*,
first published in Great Britain in 1997
by Dorling Kindersley Limited, London

Copyright © 1999 Dorling Kindersley Limited, London
Entertaining text copyright © 1997 Malcolm Hillier

Developed by Matthew A. Price, Nashville, Tennessee.

Published by C. R. Gibson®
C. R. Gibson® is a registered trademark of Thomas Nelson, Inc.
Norwalk, Connecticut 06856

Printed in Singapore by Star Standard.

ISBN 0–7667–6164–9
UPC 082272–44985–5
GB4141

PICTURE CREDITS
All food photography by Martin Brigdale, and all other photography by Stephen Hayward, with the exception of:
Steven Wooster 39 top center.

THE FOLLOWING KINDLY LOANED PROPS FOR PHOTOGRAPHY
THOMAS GOODE & CO. (LONDON) LTD.
19 South Audley Street, London W1Y 6BN
For serving dishes, plates, cutlery, glasses, and place mats used on pages 21 and 25.

VILLEROY & BOCH
267 Merton Road, London SW19 5JS
For glasses, cutlery, and plates used on pages 26–27.